CHRISTMAS IN THE *SOUTHWEST*

Holt, Rinehart and Winston / New York / Chicago / San Francisco

CHRISTMAS IN THE SOUTHWEST

Photographs by Taylor Lewis, Jr.
Text by Joanne Young

ACKNOWLEDGMENTS

The authors are grateful to the Southwesterners who shared their knowledge of the area and their Christmas customs with us. In Texas, our special thanks to Miss Marylee Battiato, Mrs. Sharon Eason, San Antonio; the J. M. McDonalds, Mission; Miss Lena Sturges, Bill Brandon, and A. G. O'Brien, Kerrville; Mrs. Letycia Palacio and the Robert O'Connors, Laredo; in New Mexico, to the Bud Lewises, Albuquerque; Mrs. Barbara Egan, the Walter L. Goodwins, Jr., and Miss Audean Davis, Santa Fe; in Arizona, to the Ed Worsleys and Mrs. Betty Krause, Phoenix; the Hermosa Inn, Scottsdale; in California, to Ruth and Harrison Brent and Mrs. Parley Johnson, Downey.

Library of Congress Cataloging in Publication Data

Lewis, Taylor Biggs.
Christmas in the Southwest.
1. Christmas—Southwest, New.
I. Young, Joanne B. II. Title.
GT4986.S64L48
394.2'68282'0979 73-3701
ISBN 0-03-010741-5

Published simultaneously in Canada by Holt, Rinehart and Winston of Canada, Limited.

First Edition
Designer: Winston Potter
Printed in the United States of America

BRIGHT with December sun, the great Southwest basks in a holiday mood from the lush Rio Grande Valley in Texas, across New Mexico's rugged mountains and the vast cactus garden of Arizona desert, to the flowering southern California coast. South of the sleepy Rio Grande, Mexico tunes her guitars and fashions her paper flowers for fiesta.

Christmas approaches in a twinkle of lights, a blaze of poinsettias, and the captivating rhythm of dancing feet. It is a festival blending the rich mix of cultures woven into the colorful fabric of the Southwest itself—Indian, Spanish, Mexican, and that of the nineteenth-century pioneers who rolled westward with the best-loved customs of many European nations to adapt to this new land.

The brilliant bloom of poinsettias in Mission, Texas, sets the stage for Christmas.

Texas—you get the feeling that everything really *is* bigger here: the grapefruit, the oil wells, the steers, the stetsons, and even the Christmas spirit! Or maybe it only seems that way under the wide blue Texas sky. It stretches endlessly over a land where you can ride for miles through mesquite and sagebrush and live oaks with only the arch above an occasional ranch gate to mark a human habitation. The illusion—if it is an illusion—is enhanced by the fact that within the Lone Star State each region is as different from the other as a bluebonnet is from a bougainvillaea vine. The rolling

The Steves Homestead in San Antonio reflects the German Yule customs that enrich Texas traditions.

plains and prairies of the north, the mountainous west, the sophisticated metropolitan areas around Dallas and Fort Worth, the historic Brazos Valley just south of them, and the Gulf coast are each different countries.

In central Texas, the wind can whip across the hill country on a December day, and a light sprinkling of snow may dust fenceposts and tumbleweed. Glossy mistletoe clusters in green balls high in oak trees, ripe for cutting to decorate a Christmas party. The whitetail deer take cover until twilight, and then cautiously slip from the brush to graze on the sweet range grass.

On one of these chilly mornings, you'll see a cowboy, cradling his youngest child behind the saddlehorn, ride out to chop down a cedar for the family Christmas tree. He may have spotted it first on a hot August day when he was riding fences, checking for broken wire that would mean straying cattle. By now its branches have filled out; and it will look pretty Christmas morning with lights and tinsel and lots of red and green and gold balls. The six-year-old will find his first pair of leather boots under its branches—he was fitted for them last week, but a wink to the clerk let him think his folks weren't buying them after all. A boy's first boots are mighty big—Texas-big, you might say, even if they are only a little boy's size twelve.

The Pedernales River is lined with windmill-dotted ranches. Among them is the LBJ Ranch, which has shared the warmth of its holidays, its barbecued beef, pinto beans, and chile con queso with visitors from all over the world. From New Braunfels to Fredericksburg nestle the stone houses of Texas's early German settlers. They landed on the Gulf coast in 1845 and came up by two-wheeled oxcarts and on foot, plagued by cholera and one of the worst rainy seasons in history, while war raged between Mexico and the United States.

The following year, John Meusebach led a group of them from New Braunfels to found Fredericksburg. He made a peace treaty, which was never broken, with the Comanche Indians, on whose land they settled.

Signifying their friendliness to all who traveled the territory, the settlers named their streets from the center of town southeast, so that the combined initials spell "all welcome," and to the northwest, "come back."

By December, they were more than ready to bring a touch of Christmas at home to the new frontier. A Texas cedar or a holly tree became their Tannenbaum—bright with candles, paper chains, candy, and gilded nuts. Around the tree, with its candles lighted on Christmas Eve, the tender notes of *"Stille Nacht, Heilige Nacht"* rang out as the eyes of children glowed.

In 1848, Ed Steves, who had been a cabinetmaker in Germany, moved to San Antonio and opened a lumber and mill-working yard. In less than thirty years, his own American dream had come true. He was prosperous enough to build a splendid Victorian mansion for his family on King William Street. (The area of fine German homes near the San Antonio River was humorously referred to as Sauerkraut Bend.) A formal garden in front, a fountain on the side which he purchased at the Philadelphia Centennial Exposition, and the city's first indoor swimming pool—it was a Texas showplace.

Now the property of the San Antonio Conservation Society, which has done so much to preserve the customs and landmarks of the past, the Steves Homestead is open to the public. At Christmas, every room reflects the charm of a Victorian holiday.

A Victorian tree at the Steves Homestead holds German ornaments and tiny candles in gay profusion.

Of the twenty-six national, racial, or cultural groups who have contributed to the development of Texas, the Spanish have left one of the strongest, brightest imprints on its Christmas celebration. This is radiantly visible at the lovely old Spanish Governor's Palace.

The long, low, white-plastered building was erected in 1722 as part of the old Spanish fort, or *presidio*. After the city became the capital of the Spanish province of Texas, its governors resided here, as did Mexican officials after that country's successful revolution against Spanish rule. Here Jim Bowie courted his bride-to-be, and Moses Austin contracted with Governor Martinez to bring the first Anglo-American colonists to Texas.

A century plant bright with pears and partridges in Laredo is truly Texan!

A Mexican "tree of life" adds the touch of one more land's traditions at Christmas time.

Three wise men from Mexico at the Steves Homestead.

Facing page: *Pan dulce and candies in the dining room of the Spanish Governor's Palace in San Antonio are ready for the Fiesta Navideña.*

Candles glow in the Palace chapel where Christmas mass was heard in 1722 when the commandancia *was a Spanish fort in the Texas wilderness.*

A fire blazes on the hearth of the high, open-throated fireplace in the dining room which was the scene of gala Spanish Colonial banquets. Was it *cabrito* or roasted wild turkey that was prepared for His Excellency's Christmas dinner in the adjoining kitchen, its charcoal fire glowing in the open stone brazier?

The Palace's family chapel, the heart of all Mexican haciendas, is mentioned in the will of Mexican Governor Ignacio Perez, dated January 25, 1849: "The small room called 'of the Blessed Virgin,' will be for my daughter, Trinidad." Rare primitive wood carvings of saints (santos) look out from niches, and religious scenes painted on tin (retablos) hang from the chapel walls. Even today no Mexican home is too small to devote at least a special corner, if not a room, to family worship.

One of the most beautiful Christmas traditions of the Southwest and Mexico, from which it comes, is Las Posadas (The Inns). In symbolic pageantry, a procession reenacts the journey of Joseph and Mary to Bethlehem and their search for a room where the Baby Jesus would be born. Then, in the happy combination of reverence and gaiety typical of the Mexican people, their welcome to the inn is followed by a festive piñata party. The custom, introduced in Mexico in the 1500s by Father Diego de Soria, was adopted as readily by Southwesterners as the German Christmas tree and Santa Claus.

Along the beautiful Paseo del Rio in San Antonio, Las Posadas is combined with another delightful tradition—the Fiesta de las Luminarias. Four hundred years ago, in Spain and later Mexico, crossed piñon boughs were set ablaze on Christmas Eve to light the way for the Christ child. The custom continued until Yankee peddlers introduced brown paper wrappings and

Above left: *The spire of San Augustine Church in Laredo.*

Hundreds of luminarias line the Paseo del Rio in San Antonio as eyes and candles glow in the Las Posadas procession, ending at La Villita.

The piñata party climaxes festivities at La Villita.

long-burning candles. Today the Southwest's luminarias are candles in sand-weighted paper bags.

At dusk they reflect in the shimmering, palm-lined river with Christmas lights on shops, hotels, and sidewalk cafes. The crowd gathers in the Spanish-style courtyard of La Mansión Motor Hotel, where it takes its place behind a brown-eyed, brown-haired "angel" with tinseled wings carrying the *Ojo de Dios* (Eye of God)—crossed sticks wound in a kite shape with colored yarns. Two young girls in long white dresses carry the *misterio*, a platform bearing clay figures of the Holy Family. They start down the steps to the river walk, each person holding a lighted candle, singing a litany as they go.

A few blocks away, a boy and girl in their early teens start across an arched bridge over the river. In the blue of not-quite-dark, they glimpse the winking luminarias and the approaching line of candles. The girl's breath catches in her throat.

"Oh—Las Posadas!" she whispers. Its lights are twinkling pinpoints in her eyes. She reaches for the boy's hand, and they run lightly down the stone steps to join the age-old ceremony. In a moment of wonder it is Christmas!

"In the name of Heaven I ask for lodging," sings the crowd in Spanish at the procession's first stop. A choir inside the building replies, "No room here; go on your way." Tens of hundreds of candles shine as the pageant moves on until they reach La Villita, the restored Mexican village in the heart of the city.

Silver trumpets blow as the wrought iron gates swing open, and the choir within the plaza sings: "You are Joseph? and your wife is Mary? Enter, pilgrims; I did not recognize you."

The rejoicing marchers fill the walled plaza; and when the misterio has been placed on an evergreens covered table, the crowd of some three thousand people sinks to its knees and sings The Lord's Prayer: "Padre nuestro, que estas in los cielos . . ."

No need to tell the children what comes next! There is a sudden cry of "Now the piñata!"

Bright blue and red and yellow Star of Bethlehem Christmas piñatas are lowered on ropes in four corners of the courtyard. (The soft clay beanpots, filled with candies and tiny presents, are traditionally decorated with bright crepe paper in the forms of stars or birds or bulls or even Mickey Mouse!)

Like dozens of jumping jacks, the children wait for their turn to be blindfolded and swing the stick at the piñata. It dances tantalizingly just out of reach. One blonde six-year-old just misses, and they squeal their disappointment. At last, with a mighty swat, a small boy connects with the target; and candy showers down like a shattered rainbow. What a shout! What a scramble! The excitement is ear-splitting as every child dives for his share.

When the last bit of crepe paper has fluttered to the ground, the last piece of candy has been claimed, there is hot chocolate and buñuelos—the crisp, lacy Mexican Christmas cookies—for everyone in the crowd. A flamenco guitarist plays, and a lovely Spanish dancer twirls and flirts through her black lace mantilla. Exuberant shouts of *"Feliz Navidad!"* mingle with "Merry Christmas!" in one joyous international carol.

For three days of the pre-Christmas holiday, "SALT's Off Stage" riverboat of the San Antonio Little Theater is "on stage" at points up and down the Paseo del Rio.

Rowdy and religious by turn, like the Elizabethans they emulate, the cast presents a modern verse adaptation of *The Second Shepherd's Play*, a medieval miracle drama. The barge drawn up to the river's edge substitutes for the

A riverboat is the stage for Los Pastores, a modern version of a miracle play.

Piñatas for sale are a sure sign of Christmas in Nuevo Laredo, Mexico.

horse-drawn wagon platform on which it was originally performed on holidays in merry old England. Their audience is equally informal, made up of Christmas shoppers, tourists, Air Force men on leave, or school children on vacation. They join in when the players sing familiar carols, wave as another riverboat goes by, and clap as enthusiastically as any first-night audience on Broadway.

On the other side of town, near *El Mercado* (the Public Market), there is a great air of excitement as streets are roped off, and merchants prepare for the Fiesta Navideña. Pizzinni's Spice Shop is a fragrant hub of activity where children buying chocolate, pralines, pumpkin or cactus candy vie with señoras shopping for the ingredients for tacos, buñuelos, and all the mouth-watering specialties that fiesta-goers will buy. The aroma of *pan dulce,* sweet, light holiday pastries in infinite variety, wafts through the open door of Mi Tierra Cafe and Bakery where the Cortez brothers act as a clearing house for news of the evening's events.

Strolling mariachis will play and sing until dawn, and there will be a blessing of the pets, piñatas, and arts and crafts for sale.

At Pizzinni's, Mrs. Henry Guerra, Sr., whose father founded the store in 1893, observes the preparations thoughtfully. "This is what we must bring back to America," she says in warm approval, "these traditions—this heritage. This is what made America great, and we need them to keep it great."

Mrs. Guerra, Jr., agrees, for she has watched a successful exchange of cultures firsthand. "Here is this Italian in the nineteenth century who comes over to America and marries a pretty girl from Durango, Mexico. And what happens? I'll tell you what happens! Today, two generations later, we're eating spaghetti *con mole!*" Her thoroughly American twins, rushing by to take two piñatas to a customer, grin their approval. Doesn't everyone flavor their spaghetti sauce with chocolate?

Candy made of pumpkin, cactus, or chocolate is a specialty at Pizzinni's Spice Shop in San Antonio.

In the tropical Texas valley, where tourists and Canada geese are winter visitors and the Mission Garden Club holds an annual Christmas Poinsettia Show, citrus groves are like no others. Their boundaries are marked by rows of royal palms, a custom dating back to a time when palm trees were more plentiful than wood for fence posts in the valley.

Dawn breaks over the Rio Grande River at Laredo, with

South of the border, in Mexico itself, festivities which started on Guadalupe Day in mid-December are now in full swing. The market places in Reynosa, Nuevo Progreso, Laredo, and Juarez—always a mecca for tourists, are even more frantically busy with Christmas shoppers. The traffic on International bridges across the Rio Grande rushes in both directions. (You can walk across for a penny.) Mexicans shop for bargains in Texas stores, while Texans find them in Mexico!

Shoeshine boys and paper flower vendors are everywhere, and sidewalk salesmen offer their wares, from serapes to steer horns. Steam puffs up from tubs of roasted corn on two-wheeled carts, and charcoal braziers in the open

Mexico lying beyond and Texas bordering it on this side.

fronts of butcher shops send out a fragrant advertisement. The raucous sound of horns blown by fearless cab drivers are syncopated by the clip-clop of burros' hoofs.

Strings of garlic and red and green peppers decorate vegetable stalls, while bins hold red, white, and speckled beans in a colorful mosaic. On one corner of a tiled sidewalk, a vendor sells fresh fruit—tangerines, slices of papaya and pineapple—to grinning children who rush up to hand him their pesos like American youngsters greeting a Good Humor man.

Through the wrought iron gates of private homes, you catch a glimpse of courtyards where bougainvillaeas bloom and Christmas tree lights shine through the windows. Wreaths hang on gates and

doors and windows, and elaborate *nacimientos* (nativity scenes), some of them life-size, decorate yards or patios.

In dozens of shops, bright tree ornaments are for sale. There are gaily painted tin angels, stars or flowers, handmade figures of straw, and white birds with paper wings and candlewax bodies.

Corn husks are a very large sales item, much in demand at this season. In many Mexican homes on both sides of the border, tamale making is at its height on Christmas Eve. Dozens and dozens are made for families and friends, most of them filled with the traditional mixture of pork, spices, and chile, but some made with chicken; or raisins and chopped fruit for a special dessert. And how could you possibly make tamales without corn husks to wrap them in for steaming?

Christmas cards in a Nuevo Laredo store window, and a nacimiento (below) in the yard of a Mexican home in the town of Roma, Texas.

The town square in Nuevo Laredo is a great spot for flower vendors, shoe shine boys, tired shoppers.

In Mexican homes, hundreds of hot tamales are made on Christmas Eve, just as they were for Spanish Governors.

The old Longhorn Saloon is a San Antonio museum now, but the Lone Star Brewery keeps beer on tap.

Surrounded by so many Yuletide customs older than the United States itself, it is hard to remember that the days of the Old West are comparatively recent. Many Southwesterners learned about cattle drives along the Chisholm Trail, range wars, and covered wagons rolling westward not from school books but from the reminiscences of older members of their families. At the turn of the century, Christmas meant family reunions, as it does today, and tales told and retold of round-up time, sourdough bread and chuck wagon meals, Indian raids, and outlaws.

Landmarks keep the Wild West alive, such as the Buckhorn Saloon, which originally stood on Houston Street in San Antonio, bright with poinsettias and gold tinsel. Once a favorite gathering place for ranchers and oil men (it had a cabinet in which cowboys were asked to hang their guns while they drank), it is now a museum. Teddy Roosevelt propped his foot on the old brass rail when he stopped in during a trip to recruit his Rough Riders; and Sam Rayburn's famous ten gallon hat hangs on the wall.

Chile con carne and tamales are the spicy favorites on the menu at the gala Christmas celebration at Mission San José. All the color and laughter, reverence and drama of the season are combined at the "Queen of Missions" which had its first celebration of Christ's birth in 1720.

It is chilly on this December evening as a full moon rises over the adobe walls. Colored lights are strung between the live oak trees, and bonfires are ringed with spectators warming cold hands and toes. On the outdoor stage, young lariat twirlers display their skill; boys and girls of the parish perform the delightful Mexican folk dances of their ancestors; while young Indians keep alive their own rich heritage with matachines dances that are at once an expression of worship and dazzling pageantry.

The history of Texas beef cattle, from the Longhorn at the top to the Hereford, is dramatically displayed at The Stockman restaurant in downtown San Antonio.

A Las Posadas begins at Mission San José y San Miguel de Aguayo (known as the Queen of Missions).

A mariachi mass blends the voices of the mission choir with guitars and trombones and the age-old sacred words.

Matachines Indian dancers and Mexican folk dancers bring color and rhythm to the Mission's Christmas celebration.

Within the chapel, a mariachi mass is celebrated. A choir wearing magnificent serapes sings of the recurring Christmas miracle while the mariachis' guitars and trombones add a rich accompaniment. The congregation leaves the church carrying candles in a Posadas procession to the creche on the stage.

Then the centuries blend as an old and primitive pageant begins. *Los Pastores* is a mystery play which was first presented in Texas missionary settlements in the early 1700s. The drama was handed down by word of mouth from generation to generation. Indian imagery and Mexican folklore were added to the original Spanish script, but it still depicts the eternal conflict between good and evil. An interpreter translates for the audience as the players speak their lines in Spanish. But as the Devil tries to keep the shepherds from reaching Bethlehem, and they defeat him, the meaning is clear.

The shepherds tap their crooks, and their small bells ring in unforgettable rhythm. They sing as the pageant ends:

Good-by, beloved Child,
    Your little shepherds are leaving;
Now close those beautiful eyes
    And go back to sleep.

New Mexico

—they call it The Land of Enchantment, and at the Christmas season, it could be named The Land of Enchanted Lights. Nowhere in the Southwest, where the Yuletide season has a glow like no other part of the country, does it shine more brightly than in New Mexico. It twinkles with starlight and candle flame, gleams with golden luminarias and farolitas, shines with colored lights that outline trees and houses. In the Santa Fe area, a luminaria refers to a Christmas bonfire, while the paper bags with candles inside, which the rest of the Southwest calls luminarias, are known as farolitas—"little lamps."

At Raton, the hills are aglow in Climax Canyon, where rocks, cedars, and piñon trees surround the lighted nativity scenes which are known as the "City of Bethlehem." Farther south, at the little town of Jemez Springs, a forty-foot living Christmas tree sparkles; luminarias flicker on rooftops; and on the hillsides, Christmas scenes handmade by the families in the area are brilliantly illuminated.

In New Mexico where mountains, caverns, mesas, and deserts all speak of antiquity, it is fitting that Christmas customs date back four hundred and fifty years to the

arrival of the first Christians. (Alvar Nuñez Cabeza de Vaca of Spain; Estévanico, a black Moor; and two other Spaniards were shipwrecked on the Texas coast in 1528 and were the first to traverse the Southwest. In an unbelievably arduous eight-year walk, they finally reached the Gulf of California and Sonora.)

To the Indian performing his Christmas deer dance at Tesuque Pueblo or the matachines dancer at Taos, even the span of time since the Europeans' coming is no more than a trickle of desert sand. For centuries before that, his ancestors held their ceremonial dances at this season, to pray for the return of the winter sun after

Under the wide starry sky of New Mexico, an adobe ranch house is lighted with golden luminarias.

At Rancho Encantado near Santa Fe, enchilladas, roast beef, Indian bread are on the Southwestern Yuletide menu.

its annual withdrawal. Now at many pueblos the Indian dances for the Christ child after midnight mass in the mission church. He does so without conflict; for he recognizes the natural clock of the universe, and this has always been a time for dancing.

Nowhere, perhaps, have the Anglo, Spanish, and Indian cultures blended so easily as in the happy customs of Christmas. With them are mixed the influence of the Southwest itself—the gay strings of red peppers, called *ristras,* on the door; the Zuñi basket filled with pine and holly; a cedar wreath hanging over a Navajo blanket in the den; English carols played on a Spanish guitar.

On Christmas dinner tables, the juicy prime ribs of beef or roast turkey are surrounded by platters of enchilladas, guacamole salad, and a hearty casserole of pinto beans. The loaves of homemade Indian bread baked in a pueblo's beehive oven are as often part of the menu as feather-light *sopaipillas*—little popovers dripping with wild honey. Dessert may be a German chocolate cake, English apple pie, or sugary *biscochitos*—the crisp Spanish Christmas cookies.

Christmas means candles—in all shapes and sizes.

Even a rare three-hundred-year-old Penitenté cross at Rancho Encantado is decked in greens and ribbon.

At La Mesita ranch outside Santa Fe, primitive santos hang above an old Spanish shepherd's bench.

The snow-covered terrain along the road to Taos has changed very little

The trader who drove his mule train from Missouri down the Santa Fe Trail in the 1800s may have shocked the housewives of Independence when he went back and demanded his eggs scrambled with green chile peppers! At any rate, much more was traded than furs and silver, tea and trinkets on the Santa Fe Trail; and in New Mexico today it's apparent that it was a valuable exchange.

The city of Santa Fe seems to have grown out of the earth itself. Its brown adobe buildings (none more than three stories high by city ordinance) seem carved out of the mountainous plateau from which the city rises. Cottonwoods line the streets and shade the secluded patios. They have probably done so since the old Palace of the Governors was built by Don Pedro Peralta in 1610, a decade before the Pilgrims set foot on Plymouth Rock. The oldest government building in the United States, the adobe wall around it enclosed not only the governor's rooms, a powder storeroom, and chapel, but quarters for soldiers and a corral for their horses. This fascinating old structure on the Plaza now houses exhibits of two millennia of New Mexican events, as part of the Museum of New Mexico.

since Alvarado searched here for the Seven Cities of Cibola in 1540.

At this time of year, its halls echo the footsteps of the ghosts of countless Christmases Past. Men and women who served there under five flags—Spanish, Mexican, American, and briefly, the Pueblo Indians (1680–1692) and the Confederacy (1862)—have each in their own way paused in late December to celebrate this holiday. Among them was Lew Wallace, who wrote his classic *Ben Hur* in the Palace while he was New Mexico's territorial governor.

At the Rancho Encantado, north of Santa Fe, thirty youngsters are bubbling with excitement as they wait for Santa Claus. The guest ranch, on a quarter section of chaparral country bordering Pojoaque Indian land, holds an annual Christmas party for youngsters eight-to-ten years old from nearby Guadalupe School.

Tantalizing spicy smells of dinner drift through the kitchen door, and dancing eyes reflect the fire on the hearth and the twinkling lights of the Christmas tree.

"I think I hear sleigh bells!" exclaims Mrs. Barbara Egan, their hostess.

"Hey, I think I do, too!" cries an excited nine-year-old, and his classmates echo him. "I think they're on the roof!"

Snow adds its own brush to a Taos artist's window.

Thirty pairs of eyes turn to the ceiling above the fireplace, and there through the skylight—one of them spies a jovial white-whiskered face.

"It's Santa Claus!" they shout. "El Santo Closs!"

The skylight slides open, and a pair of boots (suspiciously resembling cowboy boots) dangles through. Someone brings a ladder, and Santa descends with his bulging pack. The sleigh bells jingle merrily outside, and laughter rings within.

(A few days later, a group of profusely illustrated thank-you notes arrive from Guadalupe School. "Dear Mrs. Egan," writes one little boy. "Thank you for telling us you heard Santa Claus. We might have missed him otherwise.")

A few miles south of Santa Fe, two ghost towns swing silent doors to the December winds, mute testimony that man leaves only a transient mark on the landscape. Madrid, once a prosperous mining community known for its Christmas decorations, lies deserted, a billboard proclaiming that the entire town is for sale. The rows of hillside houses, the Mineshaft Tavern, the school, the church, an off-Broadway theater (a long *long* way off Broadway!) that once wore Christmas lights in gay profusion, are now as barren as a well that has run dry. A roadrunner, grown unaccustomed to the sight of human beings, strolls instead of running down the main road.

Cerillos (the Little Hills) a few miles down the road is slightly better off. The Schmidts, one family holding out against time in a neat little adobe house, have put

The chapel at the old Taos Pueblo wears a green wreath.

luminarias along the wall and a sign proclaims to all who pass, "Feliz Navidad!"

The town was founded in 1879 when the railroad first came through, opening up the turquoise, copper, silver, and gold mines to a rich eastern trade. But the mines must have given out, for L'Église de San José looks almost deserted, and the Tiffany Saloon has a message scrawled across its windows: "Sorry—closed till Easter." There appear to be more stray dogs along the dusty streets than human inhabitants. Still, the Metropolitan Hotel has a tinsel-decked tree in its lobby, and the sign as you leave town says *Hasta la Vista*, so there are at least a few hopeful residents.

Twentieth-century travelers speed along the route of the Camino Real (the Royal Road) through the Rio Grande Valley at Christmas time. Their destination differs, however, from the traders, missionaries, or soldiers who journeyed this way to and from Mexico City in the Spanish Colonial era.

Today they head for the powdery ski slopes of the Sandia or Sangré de Cristos ranges, or take off cross-country into the Pecos Wilderness. Just riding up a ski lift is a breathtaking experience. (If the altitude doesn't take your breath away, the scenery will!)

Handcrafted gifts from the nearby Indian pueblos are eagerly sought by Christmas shoppers in Albuquerque.

Indian boys sweep snow off the roof at Taos Pueblo.

Facing page: *An outdoor mural in Albuquerque's Old Town depicts the colorful early history of New Mexico.*

Seemingly endless miles of snow-covered, pine-dotted ridges and valleys spread out below, where deer and bighorn mountain sheep are in their element.

To skiers or travelers home-bound for the holidays, the road to Taos unfolds its panoramic beauty as it did to Captain Hernando de Alvarado in 1540. This officer in Coronado's expedition found several thousand Indians living in the eight hundred terraced rooms at Taos Pueblo. Instead of the legendary Seven Cities of Cibola with walls of gold, the Spaniards glimpsed adobe pueblo walls reflecting the morning sun. These well-established Indian civilizations had existed for more than fifteen centuries. The Taos people were already masters of the art of irrigation, and their fields produced abundant crops of corn, beans, and squash. Other nearby Indian tribes had skilled craftsmen—basket weavers, pottery makers, workers in silver and turquoise.

In spite of the stormy years between, the ancient arts are not only still alive but flourishing. At the Christmas season, handcrafted gifts of exquisite jewelry, intricately designed, and woven rugs, famous Nambé silver, and black-on-black potteryware from San Ildefonso are in particular demand. Christmas shoppers crowd the trading posts. Sidewalk displays do a thriving business in Albuquerque's Old Town and the ancient Plaza in Santa Fe.

Taos is a mecca for artists. Like Santa Fe, its narrow streets and softly rounded adobe buildings seem like a painting themselves.

Snow has added its magic brush to the ropes of evergreens, the nacimientos, the spruce and holly wreaths. In the town square, a group of little Indian children, bundled up from boots to parkas, are putting finishing touches on a rotund snowman. The window of an artist's studio frames an abstract painting, and the pungent scent of burning piñon logs drifts on the wind. The warmth of Christmas is in the air, and it helps to dispel the temperature's chill.

The weather is milder in Albuquerque on Christmas Eve. Early in the day, trucks begin to deliver thousands of luminarias which will line the streets, sidewalks, balconies, and roofs of Old Town. As they are put in place, workers move along the rows placing a vigil candle in each one, nestling it carefully in the sand.

The sun sets in a sky gaudy with color, fading from purple to rose to palest pink. The gaslights around the Plaza flicker. One by one, candles are lighted in the luminarias on the quaint Victorian bandstand, the shops, and San Felipe de Neri Church. In the window of La Placita Restaurant, red lights wink on a white Christmas tree, decorated entirely with red chile peppers.

Now in the last rays of the sun, the Plaza has a golden aura, jeweled with the deeper gold of the luminarias. As though on signal, a crowd begins to gather, walking along the sidewalks in the glow of a Southwestern Christmas.

When it is fully dark, a caravan of cars begins to move through the residential areas, interspersed with buses provided by the Chamber of Commerce for visitors at local inns and hotels. Headlights are dimmed; horns silent. For the most part, it is a quiet crowd, hushed by the beauty of the little lanterns; but children in lighted homes along the way merrily call out Christmas greetings to the passersby.

If Christmas is a visual thing, then in New Mexico it is a golden luminaria saying "Welcome—come in!" to the Christ child and all those who celebrate His birth.

Since 1706 Christmas Eve mass has been held at San Felipe de Neri Church in Old Town, Albuquerque. Nearby homes and streets glow with luminarias.

Arizona—on an early December morning, the air is soft as the down of a cottonwood tree. Breathe deeply, and it is heady like a fine clear wine, not too dry nor too sweet. The hills may be veiled in blue mist until the sun reaches golden fingers into the valleys. Then the desert comes richly alive, teeming with bird and animal life. It is fragrant with its special scents of creosote and flowers and sand that hold remembered heat from yesterday's sun, even the delicate aroma that water has, carried on a desert breeze.

Jackrabbits romp like gazelles. A horned toad blinks gently at the landscape like some tiny Socrates; and roadrunners begin their comical track races for the day. Cactus wrens dart from hidden nests; and

Sabino Canyon, northeast of Tucson in the Santa Catalina Mountains, holds all the delights of a desert garden.

mockingbirds, tired from their elaborate midnight serenades, hunt out the shade of a paloverde tree to rest.

To the north, the Grand Canyon is stilled in majestic snowy splendor; the Painted Desert is quiet as a frozen rainbow; and in the Navajo's Monument Valley, the buttes sculpted by time stand sentinel.

Arizonans have a great fraternity. It cuts across all lines and makes them brothers. Its members are all those who think Arizona is the greatest—in fact, the *only*—place in the world to live! They do not recruit members. It is becoming too sadly apparent that the more the clan grows, the more Arizona takes on the formerly unfamiliar evils of urban civilization with its smog and traffic. But for those who succumb to the siren call of peacocks roosting in trees at dusk, orange blossoms sending out perfume by moonlight, purple hills, and most of all, a life style deliberately unsophisticated and free from pretense, the fraternity opens its arms.

Near Tucson, at San Xavier del Bac, the beautiful Spanish mission known as the White Dove of the Desert, the Christmas season really begins on December 3, the feast day of San Xavier.

The chapel bells at San Xavier are framed by the graceful wrought-iron gate, the ocotillo and cholla. The mission was named by Father Eusebio Kino in 1692.

Near Tucson, on the Papago Indian reservation, stands San Xavier del Bac, the White Dove of the Desert.

Inside, the mission has been lovingly decorated for Christmas, its angels dressed in starched white lace robes.

From Squaw Peak, sunrise is golden over Phoenix.

As the day approaches, the Papago Indian women of the parish carefully launder the colorful, elegant vestments in which they dress the statues of the saints. They starch and press the exquisite lace robes for two angels suspended on the arch at either side of the altar, and tie red velvet capes around the lions that were modeled after the Spanish Lions of Navarre. In the angels' hands they place green satin banners emblazoned in gold with the words first sung over Bethlehem's hills—"Gloria in Excelsis Deo."

When all is in readiness, special services are held in the chapel, and three days of music, dancing, and all the traditional processions and pageantry of fiesta time begin.

Father Eusebio Francisco Kino named the mission for Saint Francis Xavier when he first visited the Sobaipuris Indian village of Bac (meaning springs) in 1692. Five years later he reported that the foundations were laid for "a very capacious church and house of San Xavier del Bac." The great missionary-explorer was a totally new type in an era when Spanish soldiers, who accompanied a priest on expeditions purportedly to convert the Indians, usually pursued gold more arduously than souls, often with murderous effect. Father Kino mapped the entire southwestern Arizona region, explored an overland route to California, and discovered the ruins at Casa Grande of a Hohokam civilization which were then already seven hundred years old. He established ranches in several areas and taught the Papago and Pima Indians to raise cattle and grow the grain to feed them.

After the death of the resident priest in 1702, the little mission was largely unattended until the arrival of another Jesuit, Father Alonso Espinosa, in 1756. He built a convent which is still in use, but the present mission was not begun until about 1781 under the direction of the Franciscan father, Juan Bautista Verderrain.

With Indian workers, he fashioned the walls of fired adobe.

On the outskirts of Mesa, sheep and new lambs graze.

They were then sheathed in plaster which was whitewashed with a combination of limestone, from nearby pits, and cactus juice. This mixture is still applied every three years to keep the graceful old building a dazzling white under the desert sun.

There are many stories as to why only one tower was completed. Some say it was to avoid the Spanish tax on finished churches; some blame it on workmen, superstitious after one of their number fell to his death while working on it; and others say the money simply ran out.

The fortunes of the White Dove waxed and waned a number of times in the next two centuries. In one period it was almost abandoned, and weather and neglect began to take their toll. Indian parishioners had to take the mission's furnishings into their homes to preserve them from vandals. In the past three decades, however, scrupulously careful restoration has preserved and enhanced its ancient beauty.

Moonlight spills mystically over its domes, its balustraded walls and arched gates on a December night. Within, its frescoed ceiling is gray with the smoke of countless votive candles, and its niches and vaulted ceiling are filled with the breath of a million prayers.

In the Holy Land, the first Christmas morning may have dawned much as it does in the Valley of the Sun in which Phoenix is located. Light rims the hills first and then the tops of palm trees, and gradually drifts down to pastures where sheep are grazing.

Sun sparkles on the gold and crimson decorations that line Phoenix streets—Santa Claus wearing a sombrero, and a sunburst that has become the Valley's symbol. In Scottsdale it smiles on three saguaro cactus wearing the robes and crowns of the Three Kings. Homes, guest ranches, and shopping centers twinkle with lights on olive trees, century plants, and all manner of cactus. Obviously, you don't need a spruce or a pine tree to get the Christmas spirit!

In downtown Phoenix Santa wears a gay sombrero.
Left: *A desert home in Lincoln Hills has a red tree.*

A tumbleweed tree is built on Chandler's town square.

Only in the Southwest will you find Three Kings who are really saguaro cactus. These are in Scottsdale.

In the town square of Chandler stands a "tree," as high as the roofs of surrounding shops, made entirely of tumbleweed! At night it shines with brightly colored lights and a golden star on top. Santa Claus has a stopping-off place at the base of the tree. Between his other chores before December 25, he takes note here of the gifts Chandler children hope to find in their stockings Christmas morning.

He also checks in at a number of homes in Phoenix where parents or grandparents have gotten word to the North Pole that a particular small girl or boy is listening for reindeer hoofs and hoping Saint Nick will make a personal visit.

A Christmas cookie dance is in full swing at the Phoenix Saddle Club.

In this project, he seems to be assisted by gentlemen whose usual occupations are not toy-making at all, but run instead to such vocations as selling insurance, teaching school, or growing cotton or grapefruit. But that's Christmas!

It's holiday party time, and the Phoenix Saddle Club is holding their "cookie dance" in the clubhouse that members built themselves. The moose head above the mantel is even wearing Christmas lights on his antlers for the occasion! Members arrive in their newest and brightest square dancing clothes—full-skirted dresses that swirl out like paper parasols, and rodeo shirts often colorfully embroidered and worn with a *bola* (a western tie of silver-tipped braided leather).

The ladies arrange the choicest cookies from their Christmas baking (the recipes were brought with them from Ohio or Iowa or Pennsylvania or Georgia) on a table close to the coffee pot. Then Johnny Schultz, the caller, starts the toe-tapping music and announces: "Choose your partners." The dancers move quickly into sets around the floor—teen-agers, gray-haired grandparents, the college professor, the lady gas-station attendant. It's "Allemande right" and "Left square through" or "Rollaway with a half sashay." It sounds like another language, but it's clear to the smiling dancers.

Do sa do your corner, girl,
Come back home and swing and whirl!

It's a good old Southwestern custom; and as they say that "Square dancing is friendship set to music," it's a natural part of this happy season!

On Wilder road in Phoenix, even the mailboxes are decorated. Santa Claus doesn't need snow to make his rounds.

California — the Golden State—stretches out along the blue Pacific for 840 miles. In the south, the cliffs that overlook the beaches, the parks, the yards of modest homes or huge estates all seem, in December, to be part of a lush tropical garden. It is hard, if not impossible, for a wreath on a door or a tree hung with tinsel icicles to compare in beauty to the profusion of roses, the exotic Bird of Paradise flowers, the date palms and banana trees on every hand. Crimson poinsettias bloom, and pyracantha and holly trees put out their brightest berries in celebration of the season. Nature herself has decorated the state for Christmas, and Californians have taken her hint as they look to New Year's for the holiday's climax with the Tournament of Roses.

Whimsical Mexican ornaments, all made of straw, trim this tree in Downey.

Just in time for Christmas the exotic Bird of Paradise bursts into bloom and seems ready to take flight.

Sun sparkles on a crimson Christmas tree among the palms at Shelter Island.

"Red hot pokers" frame a view of Laguna Beach where waves break gently on the white sandy cove below.

While most ocean-front roads along the southeastern coast of the United States are on a low flat coastal plain, in southern California, the highway hugs a cliff-top. Rolling waves break whitely on half-moon beaches, and fishing and pleasure boats, from the traveler's vantage point, look like toy ships floating on a lily-pond.

As the sun sets, the water turns to an unbelievable turquoise, almost luminescent in the pearly light. Keeping your eyes seaward, it is almost possible to forget the miles of urban sprawl, the oil wells, and the traffic, which mark the twentieth-century coast.

How different it must have looked to Juan Rodríguez Cabrillo —who had put out from Navidad (Christmas), Mexico—when he sailed into San Diego Bay in 1542 and claimed the land for the king of Spain. Or to Sir Francis Drake in 1579 when he cruised the Cali-

fornia coast and marveled at its beauty, its climate, and its natural harbors.

Today there is a special enchantment to those waters at Christmas time when marinas are a fairyland of lights that outline the mast and rigging of even the smallest boat. The great gray Navy ships are gaily decorated, and they ride at anchor off Coronado like Christmas islands floating in the Bay.

In spite of the treasures of the past which California holds in profusion—the lovely eighteenth-century Spanish missions, San Diego's Old Town with its historic homes and buildings, the old Customs House and Presidio at Monterey among them, its mushrooming growth gives the state a "new"

Ice flowers are in bloom for the holidays on a hill overlooking San Diego Bay.

A holiday brunch in Downey has California's fabulous fruit in the place of honor.

look. It is still the mecca of a westward-moving population no less than when the gold at Sutter's Mill lured the forty-niners.

Among the national groups who have left their unique imprint on California's holiday customs are the Japanese-Americans for whom New Year's—*Osho Gatsu*—is the most festive day of the year. To start out with "a clean slate," thousands of Japanese families clean their houses from ceiling to garret on New Year's Eve, and every person takes a bath shortly after the clock strikes midnight. At the Buddhist Temple in Gardena, 850 members gather outside the church as a one-ton bell is tolled 108 times to cast out the 108 evil passions of the human being. New Year's Day is spent in visiting old friends, feasting on traditional foods (rice balls, black

It is the season of roses at Ranchos las Gertrudes in Downey, where a pink crepe myrtle grows from a tree brought across the plains by covered wagon all the way from Alabama in 1860.

beans, dried herring eggs, a tangerine) and exchanging toasts in sake: *"Shin Nen Omedeto"*—"Happy New Year!"

You will hear the American translation shouted back and forth along Pasadena streets on New Year's Eve, also; but here the resemblance in the two celebrations seems to end. The crowds camping out on every street along which the Tournament of Roses Parade will move the following morning, have been gathering there since noon on the day before New Year's Eve. Whole families have moved in with sleeping bags and picnic baskets, a charcoal burner in case the temperature drops, and odds and ends of paraphernalia, which transform Colorado Boulevard and surrounding sidestreets into a holiday gypsy camp.

If you are decorating a float with crepe paper, there is nothing to stop you (except possibly the lack of a building to keep it dry) from putting on the finishing touches days in advance. But if you are working with millions of fresh flower petals, the possible time lapse changes into hours! Work goes on around the clock on New Year's Eve, and the last petal may be put in place only moments before the Grand Marshal leads off

Early on New Year's Day, the Tournament of Roses Parade in Pasadena caps the Southwestern holidays.

the parade. The finished floats are works of art, unbelievable in their shading of colors and the intricacy of the figures and the illusions that can be created.

Bands play, horses are wheeled in precision formations, flags fly, pretty girls smile and smile and smile in spite of the shivering wind that may turn a bathing beauty blue by the end of the march. Celebrities wave to cheering crowds; and vendors sell color film to amateur photographers who are as numerous as the roses.

Most of all, the new year is welcomed in with a medley of fun and noise and laughter and beauty, a golden sun, and the absolute certainty that it's bound to be the happiest new year ever!

Noel
Feliz Navidad